Smart Shopping: Shopping Green

Jeanne Nagle
AR B.L.: 8.3 Alt.: 1240
Points: 1.0                    MG

**Your Carbon Footprint**™

## Smart Shopping:
# Shopping Green

Jeanne Nagle

rosen publishing's
**rosen central**®

New York

*For Dave and Deb, who make their own and do it themselves*

Published in 2009 by The Rosen Publishing Group, Inc.
29 East 21st Street, New York, NY 10010

First Edition

**Library of Congress Cataloging-in-Publication Data**

Nagle, Jeanne.
Smart shopping: shopping green / Jeanne Nagle.
    p. cm.—(Your carbon footprint)
Includes bibliographical references and index.
ISBN-13: 978-1-4042-1775-1 (library binding)
1. Environmental protection—Citizen participation. 2. Green movement. 3. Consumer education. I. Title.
TD171.7.N35 2009
640—dc22

                                                              2008010297

*Manufactured in the United States of America*

**On the cover:** Top: Smart shoppers investigate all the possibilities before they buy. Bottom: Organic produce is healthier for your body and the environment. Right: Reusable bags let you carry your purchases in green style.

# Contents

# Introduction

You have the power to save the world, and it's right in your pocket—or maybe your wallet or purse. What you buy, or choose not to buy, has a big impact on the size of your personal carbon footprint.

You see, the things you consume (meaning buy and own) contribute to the problem of global warming. It all starts with what's known as the greenhouse effect. Energy from the sun warms Earth. The planet stays warm because when the heat tries to escape back out into space, gases such as carbon dioxide keep it from doing so. This is known as the greenhouse effect, since the atmospheric gases let in sunlight but retain heat in much the same way that windows of a greenhouse keep plants warm.

When large amounts of these gases accumulate in the atmosphere, they trap too much warmth and Earth heats up more than usual, making overall temperatures rise. This is global warming. Rising temperatures change the planet's climate and can cause all sorts of problems, including an increase in weather-related disasters such as hurricanes.

The process of manufacturing and using certain items that you buy releases harmful gases into the atmosphere. Cars are a perfect example. Manufacturing the steel to create cars, which involves extremely hot-burning furnaces, spews pollutants.

Filling up your tank also helps fill the air with dangerous carbon dioxide. Burning fossil fuels like gasoline is a major cause of global warming.

And carbon dioxide is emitted when driving a car, from the burning of oil and gasoline.

Scientists believe these human-made sources of carbon dioxide are a major cause of global warming. In other words, each of us makes a contribution to global warming—called our carbon footprint—when we consume products. The way to reduce that footprint is to become a green consumer. That requires a combination of considering your purchases before buying, making do with less, and consuming goods and services that make use of recycled materials, or using materials that are energy-efficient from the start.

Being a green consumer is not always easy. You often have to search for energy-efficient alternatives to the items you would normally buy. The good news is that, because of pressure placed on them by green consumers, more and more corporations are offering products and services that are Earth-friendly and can reduce your carbon footprint. The not-so-good news is that the cost is often a bit higher for such offerings. Still, many carbon-reducing products wind up being worth the extra money because they last for a while. In the long run, you may actually save money. Besides, you can't put a price on keeping Earth whole, healthy, and able to sustain life, can you?

# Sustainable Consumption

The key to becoming a green consumer is to practice sustainable consumption. The first part of that phrase means we keep ourselves—and Earth—alive and healthy, or sustained. Consumption is the act of consuming, which refers to what we buy and use. Sustainable consumption, then, involves owning and using things in a way that will help us have a good quality of life but will also sustain Earth at the same time.

This is where reducing your carbon footprint comes into the picture. Making purchases in ways that do not carelessly use up our natural resources or contribute to the buildup of greenhouse gases is your goal. To accomplish this mission, you most likely will have to make some changes in the way you shop, as well as rethink many of the specific items you would normally buy.

## Buy Carefully and Thoughtfully

Sustainable consumption relies heavily on shoppers' ability and willingness to ask themselves questions—and answer them honestly—before plunking down cash for consumables, which are goods and services. This is thoughtful purchasing,

Smart shopping involves getting all the information you can about products so that you can make the greenest choice. Sometimes, that may mean buying nothing at all.

which is the opposite of merely buying something because you suddenly see it and want it, or because everybody else has it.

In fact, that's the first question you should ask yourself when you're shopping: Do I need this item, or do I merely want it? You can figure this out by deciding what you would do with the item, how often you'd use it, and if you already have something similar that would work just as well. If you can't determine how you'd use something, or if you decide you would use it only a couple of times before moving on to something else, then don't buy it. The same goes for purchasing duplicates. Remember, needing something holds more weight than wanting something when it comes to sustainable consumption.

Wanting stuff isn't awful or off-limits when you're a green consumer, though. You just have to ask yourself a couple of extra questions. Consider why you want the item in the first place. Would having it make your life easier or happier? Will the item still be worth its initial cost after you've owned it for a week? A month? A year? If you can truthfully answer "yes" to all of these questions, then go ahead and buy the thing you desire.

## Measuring the Footprint of What You Consume

Another factor you need to consider is the carbon footprint of the goods and services you purchase. To do this, trace the life cycle of a product, figuring out how it was made, how and over what distance it was shipped, and how it will be discarded once it is no longer useable. Each of these steps has an effect on a consumable's carbon footprint.

This may seem like an overwhelming task. The Carbon Trust, a private British company working to reduce carbon emissions, estimates that it takes a team of researchers several months to gather the emissions numbers on a single product. How could you, a single consumer, calculate the carbon emissions of everything you buy or figure out how every product will decompose when it is thrown away?

The truth is, you can't. The best you can do is estimate, or take an educated guess. To make it easy, simply focus on the three factors—manufacturing, shipping, and disposal—and how much energy they consume or how many pollutants they release. During the manufacturing

Shipping items adds to their overall carbon footprint. The more miles covered by cargo trucks used to transport products, the more carbon dioxide that is emitted into the atmosphere.

process, electricity is normally consumed, which requires the burning of fossil fuels such as coal or oil. So, a long or complex manufacturing process creates a large carbon footprint. Likewise, the greater the distance traveled during shipping (which leads to carbon dioxide emissions from gasoline exhaust), the greater the carbon footprint. As for disposal, the more processed, or changed from its natural state, an item is or the more chemicals that are used to create it, the greater the chance it will release toxic gases as it decomposes.

# A New Label for Carbon Emissions

In Britain, some companies do the measuring for you by placing carbon labels on their products. These are like price tags, but instead, they show the total carbon emissions generated to make a product, from its creation right up until it reaches the store shelf. According to a September 2007 report in the *Boston Globe*, a few companies in the United States have started labeling their products. Timberland was the first American company to do so, and major corporations such as PepsiCo and Wal-Mart are considering it as well.

Before you buy, take a moment to find out if there is an alternative, or another option, to the item you need that could leave a smaller carbon footprint. There are plenty of green alternatives to most conventional goods and services. Many of these will be discussed in chapter 2. When dealing with several green options, purchase the one with the lowest carbon footprint.

## Support Socially Responsible Companies

There is a way to reduce your carbon footprint without having to measure each product's contribution to greenhouse gases: You can obtain goods and services from a socially responsible company.

According to the U.S. Department of State's Bureau of Educational and Cultural Affairs, socially responsible businesses consider consumer satisfaction, customer and employee safety, and society's well-being in addition to making a profit. They provide goods and services that are in line with the values consumers hold dear. In this age of environmental awareness, such values include reducing our carbon footprint.

Socially responsible businesses follow a written code of ethics that acts as a guideline for all business dealings. They also have either an internal or external monitoring system to ensure they are following the code. With these safeguards in place, you can be reasonably sure that products from socially responsible businesses are environmentally friendly.

## Carbon Offsets

There are items you can add to your shopping list that will help you reduce your carbon footprint no matter what the circumstances. You can buy carbon offsets. These are investments in programs and projects that are designed to reduce carbon dioxide emissions. To offset something means you are making up the difference; a carbon offset helps make up the difference in emissions produced by products you may have purchased that are not very efficient in their use of energy and resources.

One of the most common carbon offsets involves planting trees, which filter carbon dioxide emissions from the air. However, it takes several years for trees to mature enough to effectively filter the emissions, so they are called low-quality offsets. High-quality offsets, which provide more immediate results, include alternative energy sources such as wind farms.

According to a 2006 report by Clean Air–Cool Planet, carbon offsets generally cost anywhere from five to twenty-five dollars each, depending

Planting trees, which soak up carbon dioxide and filter it out of the air, is one way to offset the greenhouse gases your shopping habits produce.

on the seller. The average cost is about ten dollars. For each offset you buy, you will receive a certificate. There are many carbon offset vendors, or sellers. A nonprofit group called the Climate Trust (ClimateTrust.org), whose sole purpose is to provide offset information and opportunities, would be a good place to start if you are interested in purchasing carbon offsets.

Keep in mind that carbon offsets are not a free pass to ignore your efforts toward sustainable consumption. They are merely an extra way that you can make your consumer dollars work toward reducing your carbon footprint.

## Power Shopping

According to the investment bank Adams, Harkness & Hill, the number of U.S. consumers looking to buy eco-responsible products has been rising for years. Recent sales figures seem to confirm this. In 1998, sales of green products were at just about $14.8 billion. A mere five years later, that number had more than doubled, to $36 billion. The demand for green goods and services continues to grow. As a result, a large percentage of American companies now offer greener versions of products that people use every day.

What does this mean for you as a sustainable consumer? Well, it should give you a justifiable feeling of power! Businesses both large and small depend on consumer dollars to keep them afloat. Because they don't want to lose customers and would like to gain new ones, they spend a lot of time and money investigating what goods and services consumers want. Then they produce their products accordingly.

Every time you purchase in a green way, you let companies know your preferences. It's like casting a vote for products that reduce greenhouse gases, thereby keeping them on the market and encouraging the production of similar items. In other words, how you choose to spend your hard-earned money has an impact not only on the size of your personal carbon footprint, but also on the corporate footprint.

# 2 | Buy Green

To reduce your carbon footprint with regard to consumerism, think green. That means you should try to purchase items that are environmentally friendly and contribute the least to the problem of global warming. This chapter outlines some of the specific ways that you can tailor your shopping habits to help keep the planet healthy and beautiful.

## Buy Local

One of the best, and often most convenient, choices you can make for the environment is to shop in your own backyard. Buying locally reduces your carbon footprint by lessening your dependence on fossil fuel–based forms of transportation, like cars, trucks, planes, and cargo ships.

Buying local doesn't mean you go to a national chain store that happens to be a few blocks from your house. You want to seek out small businesses and individuals who make products in your area.

The idea of buying local can expand as you need it to, but not too far. In other words, if you can't find what you need in your town or city, check out what your state or province has to offer. For certain large items, like cars or major appliances, you may have to think of a "local" product as anything made in your country. The idea is to choose goods and services that originate as close to where you live as possible.

## Food for Thought

According to the Rodale Institute, an organization that seeks agricultural solutions to health and environmental issues such as global warming, each mouthful of food on American plates travels, on average, 1,400 miles (2,253 kilometers) before it is eaten. This may be partly why the most common item that green consumers in America buy locally is food. Land across the country is dedicated to farming, so it is relatively easy to find produce, eggs, milk, and meat from nearby sources. Many grocery stores carry locally grown and raised food because it's cheaper than importing items from other states or countries.

If your grocery store doesn't sell local produce (you can find out by speaking with the store manager), you still have options. Farmers' markets, for example, feature crops and other goods produced by small farms and community gardens. Another choice you can make is to shop at cooperative or natural-foods markets. These markets are known for offering a wide selection of locally produced, chemical-free, wholesome goods. Look in local newspapers or call your county agriculture department for the location of cooperatives and farmers' markets near you.

Even big cities like Chicago have farmers' markets, where bushels full of fresh, locally grown, organic produce are available.

## Chemical-Free

Another benefit of buying locally grown food is those goods are often produced by small companies that use organic growing methods. This means the food has not been exposed to harmful chemicals that can generate greenhouse gases. For produce that is not locally grown, look for labels stating the food is "USDA Organic" or "Certified Organic."

You would be wise to choose organic food over nonorganic, but know that the term "organic" means something different when it's not

# Melts in Your Mouth, Not in the Sun

Think about not only *where* but *how* your food is grown or raised when considering its impact on your carbon footprint. Certain practices and farming methods can increase the total carbon emissions associated with a product.

Take chocolate, for example. Traditional cacao plants grow best in the shade. However, because these plants bring in a lot of money, cacao farmers in the Amazon region of South America have devoted more and more land to this crop. To make way for the plants, the carbon-filtering foliage that usually shades them is destroyed, and the new crop is grown in direct sunlight. These are harsh conditions for cacao plants. So, to help them grow in this unnatural environment, farmers use lots of fertilizers and pesticides. The result of spraying these chemicals is an extra dose of dangerous greenhouse gases seeping into the atmosphere.

Luckily for all you chocoholics out there, some farmers still use the old methods to grow cacao. Look for chocolate with a "Certified Organic" label to indulge in a treat with a smaller carbon footprint.

related to food. For instance, in cleaning products, organic can also refer to natural yet potentially hazardous chemicals, including carbon-based compounds.

If you are a dedicated green consumer, concerns over dangerous chemicals should affect your clothing purchases as well. Pants, shirts, dresses, and skirts that need to be dry-cleaned should be off-limits. Dry cleaning uses chemicals, such as perchloroethylene, that have been

A label stamped with the U.S. Department of Agriculture seal means the product has met strict standards for quality.

linked to global warming. Opt instead for cotton and wool, which are natural fibers that can be machine-washed. And when you wash them, use cool or cold water in order to save the energy used to heat hot-water washes.

## Labels and Other Disclosures

Labels will help you in your quest to be a green consumer. They clue you in to a product's contents and where it was made or packaged. The first is important because some materials and chemicals are toxic in their own right. The second point indicates how far a product had to travel. The farther away an item was made, the greater its carbon footprint due to the burning of fossil fuels required in transporting the product.

In general, consumers should pay attention to any warning notices that appear on packages. These should be a red flag that a product may contain chemicals or ingredients that could be harmful to people and the environment. You should further investigate any and all products that have the words "caution" or "hazardous" on their labels.

For information not normally listed on a product's label, check its Material Safety Data Sheet (MSDS). The MSDS lists ingredients, potentially hazardous substances (as defined by the U.S. Occupational Safety and Health Administration), and other important information.

To locate a product's MSDS, look on the company's Web site, which may post this data sheet electronically. Or, find a phone number or address and contact the manufacturer directly to request a copy.

As a general rule, you should feel pretty confident about buying goods that have nothing to hide. Choose products that will give you a full list of ingredients, either on a label or through the MSDS. For items that don't normally come with labels attached, like jewelry, ask the sellers for background information on the products and any written assurances that they can give you regarding their environmental impact. Any claims made should be backed up by a reputable and trusted source such as a government agency or a consumer watchdog group.

## Reuse and Recycle

The United States has been referred to as a "disposable society." That's because many consumers in America are hooked on the convenience of products that can be used once and thrown away. Not having to clean and maintain items appeals to people.

Unfortunately, it also makes your carbon footprint larger. Disposable products by definition don't have a long life cycle; once you are through with them, you need to buy more. To meet the demand for repeat purchases of disposable items, manufacturers consume more energy to create replacements and ship them to stores. Also, there are the greenhouse gas emissions from decomposing disposable materials. True green consumers choose reusable versions of products instead, like cloth towels instead of paper towels, or ceramic or steel beverage mugs instead of paper or Styrofoam cups.

Buying recycled paper products saves energy as well as Earth's natural resources, in the form of carbon-filtering trees.

Recycling works in much the same way. It takes less energy to recycle materials for reuse than it does to create new products from scratch. Plus, you save natural resources and the energy used to harvest them in the process. Take paper as just one example. Scientists estimate that using recycled paper saves about 40 percent of the energy that is required to make a new paper product. On top of that, buying recycled tissue paper products (Kleenex, toilet paper) would save thousands of trees that help process greenhouse gases. Read the fine print on packages and labels to see if recycled materials were used. For instance, look for the words "Post-Consumer Recycled (PCR) Content" or "Processed-Chlorine Free (PCF)" on paper products.

For purchases that are not made of recycled materials, try to buy items that can be recycled after they are used. Choose plastics that have a 1, 2, or 5 stamped on them, usually on the bottom. These numbers indicate a grade of plastic that can be recycled.

Other less obvious ways to reuse and recycle include shopping at thrift and secondhand stores and buying electronics from manufacturers that have take-back policies, in which old components are collected for recycling and safe disposal.

# Paper or Plastic?

Another shopping habit you may need to change involves how you cart home all the stuff you buy. Currently, most stores package the items you purchase in either plastic or paper bags. There is a problem with both options.

Plastic bags are made from polyethylene, which is a petroleum-based product. Polyethylene produces harmful emissions and rarely degrades fully. Plastic seems to hang around forever. Plastic bags can be recycled, but consumers return only a small percentage of those for reuse.

Paper bags are made from processed tree pulp. This makes them a double threat. Not only are carbon dioxide–filtering trees destroyed, leaving more greenhouse gases in the air, but toxic chemicals such as chlorine and dye are added to the pulp. These chemicals are responsible for dangerous emissions of their own.

To reduce your carbon footprint, buy a couple of reusable cloth bags and take them with you on all your shopping trips.

## Packaging Concerns

Green consumers make it their business to know not only the contents of products, but also how and with what materials the merchandise is packaged. A majority of products available in the United States are packaged using cardboard and plastic. The problem is that producing cardboard destroys trees that filter carbon dioxide out of the air, and manufacturing plastic releases all sorts of nasty chemicals. Also, the indestructible nature of plastic—so good at keeping products from being damaged—makes it a hazard because it doesn't biodegrade, or break down naturally.

Manufacturers often wrap their products in lots of unnecessary cardboard and plastic. When you buy in bulk, you eliminate extra packaging materials.

Some manufacturers are experimenting with Earth-friendly forms of packaging such as cellophane wrap made from biodegradable cornstarch. Most companies, however, rely on the standbys listed previously. Therefore, thoughtful shoppers like you choose items packaged in materials made from recycled content or materials that can be recycled themselves, or both.

# 3 Do More with Less

A big threat to reducing your carbon footprint is what's known as conspicuous consumption. This is buying lots of stuff just to have it, and then showing off your possessions as status symbols. Unfortunately, you do more than show off when you buy a lot of stuff. You also make it possible for increased carbon dioxide and other toxic emissions to ruin the planet.

Your goal as a green consumer is the exact opposite of conspicuous consumption. You want to purchase only the items that you need because using less saves the natural resources that help sustain Earth and limits the size of your carbon footprint.

So, how do you become more of an "inconspicuous consumer"? You make a point of doing more with less. Commit to a certain lifestyle that involves living more simply and self-sufficiently. Join forces with others to make purchases and reduce everyone's carbon footprint in the process. Also, make an effort to prolong the life of that which you already have. Green consumers try to incorporate one or all of these ideas into their lives. "Traveling light" also makes you feel less weighed down and hemmed in by useless "stuff."

# Avoid Conspicuous Consumption

Figure out your priorities, or the things that are most important to you. If gaining status and approval through the things you own is more important to you than saving the planet, then you're going to have a tough time becoming a green consumer.

- Prioritize the items that you would like to purchase in terms of what's needed immediately and what can wait a while.
- Minimize the use and purchasing of goods and services that use a lot of energy, like computers, electronic games, and music players, or try to avoid long trips that burn great amounts of carbon-emitting fossil fuels.
- Make a shopping list, especially when it comes to groceries, and stick to it.
- Resist impulse purchases. Marketers frequently place luxury, or unnecessary, items in displays located in strategic areas, especially near cash registers. They're hoping you'll see the item and decide to add it to your purchases on the spot. Don't give in to the temptation.

## Living the Simple Life

Living simply does not mean doing without material goods. It means living well with less. For instance, you could own one or two pairs of jeans instead of three or more. Making sure that the rooms, basement, and closets of your house contain only practical items that you and your family use on a regular basis is another way to live simply.

Giving up luxury items and some conveniences that you've grown used to, however, is required as well. Try using a clothesline—weather and space permitting, of course—to dry your clothes instead of a machine that uses electricity. Cooking simple meals made from fresh, seasonal, locally grown food may feel more complicated than pulling up to the "drive-thru" window of your favorite fast-food restaurant, but in terms of your carbon footprint, it's actually simpler.

Living with less can mean doing without an SUV and the expensive, environmentally harmful fuel it guzzles. Instead, whenever possible, use public transportation, a bike, or a smaller hybrid car that uses less gas.

## Live Cooperatively

Reducing your carbon footprint becomes a joint effort when you choose to live cooperatively. Cooperation involves you and a group of people working together so that everyone benefits. When green consumers live cooperatively, the planet benefits, too.

If you choose to try the cooperative life, the first thing you should do is gather a group of people that you think might make a good green

Community dinners, where large groups gather to cook and eat a meal, are an excellent example of cooperative living.

team. They should be folks who, like you, care about the environment and want to reduce their carbon footprint. Your group can be large or small, made up of friends, family, neighbors, or students throughout your school. It can be formal—with rules and regular meetings, like a club—or informal.

The next thing you want to do is pool your resources. Each person in the group should make a mental, or actual, list of items that he or she already owns. Also have everyone figure out items they might want or need at that moment or in the near future. See if there is any similarity between what's on the lists. If someone in your cooperative living group has items you need, you can borrow them. Or, you might have something that someone else needs, and the two of you could arrange to swap the items, either for a short time or for keeps.

Cooperative living can also save gas money and carbon emissions by minimizing trips to and from stores. This works particularly well with groceries. Have the group agree on one day a week to go shopping and carpool to the store. Either everyone in the group could ride along, if it's a small group, or a couple of volunteers could take member lists and shop for everyone. Whenever possible, buy items in bulk and split them up among the group. This saves money as well as the carbon emissions caused by extra packaging from several single items.

## Freecycling

You can expand your cooperative living circle further when you join an online freecycling network. The term "freecycle" comes from combining the words "free" and "recycle." Networks are formed by users in different cities or states and operate like eBay, where you can search for or post items online, except there is no cost involved. Everything on the network is free.

Here's how to get started. Go to Freecycle.org, the original freecycle network started in 2003 that now acts as a network clearinghouse. Search for a network in your area and sign up. Joining is free, and it usually includes giving a username and a working e-mail address. Once you've joined, you can post either "Wanted" or "Offered" ads online.

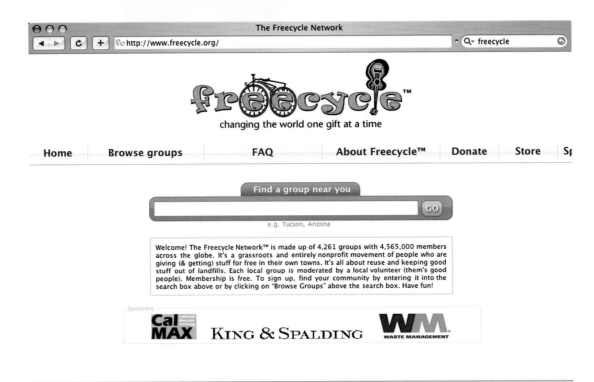

The Freecycle online network (www.freecycle.org) makes it easy to locate recycled items and give stuff you no longer use a new home.

Items can be new or "gently used," which means they're clean and in decent working order. Offerings should also be legal and appropriate for all age groups.

After another member contacts you, e-mail arrangements are made to get the item, free of charge, to the person who wants it. When picking up or delivering freecycle items, it is best to make the exchange in a neutral, public location. Never give your full name, home address, or other personal information to strangers you meet on the Web, even if they are a part of your local freecycle network. Also, make sure someone is with you—preferably an adult, but a friend could work as well—when you pick up or drop off freecycle treasures.

Freecycling is an excellent opportunity to be a green consumer in two ways. First, by choosing to own items already in existence, you eliminate the carbon emissions that making and shipping new merchandise would have created. Second, when you either give away or accept an item, you save it from rotting in landfills, which give off all sorts of toxic chemicals.

## Do It Yourself

As a consumer, you have the choice to avoid buying certain manufactured products and practice a little self-sufficiency. The do-it-yourself (DIY) approach used to be the norm. Before such conveniences as washing machines and ready-made, prepackaged meals were available, folks had to clean, cook, and perform other such tasks on their own.

Today, DIY has gained some popularity, with people making home repairs or creative gifts. But there's so much more that you, as a green consumer, can do. For instance, you can create homemade substitutes for personal-care products such as soap, toner, and lotion. You can also make your own cleaning products. The Internet and your local library have recipes and information on making your own cosmetics and body-care items. When you're just starting out, try to find formulas that aren't too complicated and try to use common, natural ingredients.

Another DIY option is clothing and accessories. This will require that you either know how or are willing to learn how to knit or sew.

When you do it yourself, you know where the materials come from, and you can be sure you get exactly what you want.

Creating your own clothing takes more work than shopping, but the benefits are being able to express your own personal style while saving the environment.

## Second Life

Green consumers wring every ounce of usefulness out of the products they buy and own. When something breaks or is outdated, you don't just replace it with a new item. First, try to either repair or upgrade what's already in your possession.

Check the Yellow Pages directory under "Repair" or by the item name and "Service" to fix anything from shoes to appliances, electronics to jewelry. Many manufacturers also offer repair services for their products. When you do have to buy something new, be sure to send in any warranty information so that you can get certain repairs for free. Also, consider purchasing the service agreement some stores offer that covers repairs past the warranty. If the agreement doesn't cost much and covers more than a year into the future, it might be worth the investment.

"Upgrading" is a term most often used with electronics. You can buy or download software for computers and cell phones that makes

## Clean and Green

Experts agree that most cleaning jobs require little more than soap, water, and a good scrubbing. If, however, you find yourself in need of something a little more powerful, you can try these natural ingredients, either by themselves or in combinations:

- Baking soda scrubs well and loosens baked-on cooking residue.
- Distilled white vinegar (not red or apple cider vinegar) cleans, removes stains, and disinfects.
- Salt is good for cleaning pots and pans.
- Club soda provides fizzy cleaning and pretreating action.
- Lemon juice cuts grease.
- Olive oil picks up dirt and polishes wood.

them function like newer models. Upgrading may not be less expensive than buying new in some cases, and it certainly takes a little more time and effort than purchasing items preloaded with the latest programs. However, it will reduce your carbon footprint.

# 4 | Become a Green Consumer Advocate

The choices you make when it comes to purchasing can definitely reduce your carbon footprint. But what about other people's footprints? You can't, and shouldn't, force anyone to lessen his or her impact on global warming. However, you might be able to influence or inspire someone to become more of a green consumer.

Advocacy is when you support a cause so strongly that your words and actions can convince others it's a good idea as well. By merely doing what you feel is right, you could shrink the impact other people have on the environment, too.

## Take Action

What you choose to buy, or not buy, says a lot about your concern for our planet. Great, but don't stop there. Seek out additional ways to let your voice be heard while you open up new avenues for green consumerism in general.

You can start by observing what environmentally friendly (organic and locally produced) merchandise is available in the stores you frequent and then contact the managers of the places that lack a sufficient selection. Try not to just drop by unannounced and ask to speak to the person in charge. It might

Check with local retailers to see if they carry green merchandise. Look for signs and labels that state products are locally made or chemical-free.

be better to introduce yourself in a letter first or make an appointment to meet at a later time, when both you and the manager are prepared for the conversation.

This can be done on your own or as part of a team formed specifically for this purpose. The key either way is persistence. Stating your case once may get a manager's attention, but it probably won't bring about the changes you want. Don't become an annoying pest, but keep speaking to managers until you notice more green options on store shelves.

# Adopt-a-Supermarket

A possible model for action is the national Adopt-a-Supermarket program of the nonprofit organization Co-op America. The program is based on the principle of fair trade, which seeks decent pay and safe working conditions for laborers around the world, as well as environmentally sound practices for creating the goods we consume.

A group of people picks, or "adopts," one store in their area, with the goal of having that store offer their customers either some or more free-trade items. Co-op America provides a free online guide to the adoption process on its Web site, www.CoopAmerica.org. Full of ideas about how you can make your adoption a success, the guide is worth a look. Simply go to the organization's home page of the site and search for "Adopt-a-Supermarket."

## Start a Petition

If meetings and letters don't seem to be working, consider starting a petition. This is a written statement that draws attention to an issue by outlining perceived problems and possible solutions. The object is to get as many people as possible to agree with the statement and sign their names as confirmation of that. The more signatures there are, the more convinced people will be that this is a serious issue.

Begin your petition with a one- or two-sentence description of the problem—in this case, an organization's lack of green products and services. You can phrase your opening so that it sounds like a request or a demand, keeping in mind that most people find it easier to go along if they are asked nicely.

Next, explain briefly but clearly why this is an issue worthy of concern. Describe global warming and its potential consequences, and point out how the merchandise that the organization offers adds to the problem. For instance, you could show how transporting produce from distant locations burns up lots of fossil fuels, which increases carbon emissions. Make sure you research your topic before you write, so you have all the facts straight and the petition does not contain errors.

Getting as many people as possible to sign a petition lets politicians and CEOs know that the issue matters to a large population, not just certain individuals.

Finally, list the specific steps that you would like to see taken to correct the problem. Be reasonable, and try to keep the list down to three to five action steps.

Because they are designed to influence people who are in a position to make changes, petitions are usually sent to the heads of companies or to politicians. Petitions can be written on paper, but the greener option would be to post them online or send them via e-mail.

## Boycott

If all else fails, you might want to try boycotting, which is refusing to do business with a person or organization as a way of protesting that person or organization's behavior and actions. The reason boycotting works is simple: When people don't buy their products, companies lose money.

When a single consumer chooses not to do business with companies that won't offer green alternative products or that promote items known to contribute to greenhouse gases, it is still called boycotting. Traditionally, though, this tactic involves convincing many people to stay away from a merchant in order to make the biggest possible impact.

Boycotting revolves around gathering and sharing information. First, research the company you plan to boycott. Make sure you have all the facts before you accuse anyone of anything. For instance, a manufacturer might produce a product that is a huge polluter but may be ready to introduce a cleaner, more eco-friendly version in the near future. Next, inform the organization that you are going to be boycotting it. The promise of such an action may be enough to bring about changes.

Finally, get the word out when you boycott so as many like-minded people as possible can join your fight. Talk about it with your friends. Write a letter to the editor of your city's newspaper explaining what you are doing and why. Post a blog or set up a Web site covering your progress.

## Worth the Effort

As you can see, being an advocate requires a lot of time, effort, and dedication—just like being a green consumer does. Changing your purchasing outlook and habits may be only one step toward reducing your carbon footprint, but it's an important one that is definitely worth the effort.

# Glossary

**advocacy**  The act of supporting a cause through one's spoken words, actions, or writing.

**alternative**  A different option.

**biodegradable**  Able to decompose through natural means.

**boycott**  To avoid dealing with a business or person as a form of protest.

**carbon footprint**  An individual's contribution to higher carbon dioxide levels.

**conspicuous consumption**  Buying products for the sake of status, not for their usefulness.

**consumer**  Someone who buys and uses goods and services.

**cooperative living**  When a group of people works together so that everyone benefits.

**emissions**  Fumes or gases that are released into the atmosphere.

**freecycling**  Offering and obtaining merchandise online, free of charge.

**global warming**  A slow but steady increase in the temperature of Earth's surface and its oceans due to carbon dioxide and other gases.

**merchandise**  Things that are bought and sold; goods; wares; commodities.

**Material Safety Data Sheet (MSDS)**  A list of a product's ingredients, potentially hazardous substances, and other important information.

**offset**  To make up for, or balance.

**organic**  From a living organism; regarding food, it means that only natural pesticides and fertilizers were used.

**petition**  A written statement that draws attention to an issue by outlining perceived problems and possible solutions. Normally, signatures are collected to demonstrate widespread agreement with this statement.

**polyethylene**  A petroleum-based product used to make plastic shopping bags.

**resource**  Something that is available for use, that can be drawn upon for aid or to meet a need; available money, property, wealth, or assets.

**sustainable**  A level of consumption that can be supplied by the environment without overtaxing it.

**toxic**  Harmful; poisonous.

# For More Information

Consumers Union
101 Truman Avenue
Yonkers, NY 10703-1057
Web site: http://www.consumersunion.org
Consumers Union, publisher of *Consumer Reports*, is an independent, nonprofit
organization that works to ensure a fair and safe marketplace for consumers.

David Suzuki Foundation
Suite 219, 2211 West 4th Avenue
Vancouver, BC V6K 4S2
Canada
Web site: http://www.davidsuzuki.org
This foundation uses science, education, and advocacy to promote solutions that
conserve nature and help achieve sustainability.

Responsible Shopper
1612 K Street NW, Suite 600
Washington, DC 20006
Web site: http://www.coopamerica.org/programs/rs
Responsible Shopper alerts the public about the social and environmental impact of
major corporations and provides opportunities for people to vote for change with
their dollars.

Union of Concerned Scientists
2 Brattle Square
Cambridge, MA 02238-9105

Web site: http://www.ucsusa.org

UCS combines independent scientific research and citizen action to develop practical solutions to environmental issues. The nonprofit also works to influence government policy, corporate practices, and consumer choices.

Zerofootprint

862 Richmond Street West, Suite 302

Toronto, ON M6J 1C9

Canada

Web site: http://zerofootprint.net

Zerofootprint provides information, products, and services to the global network of consumers and businesses that wish to reduce their environmental impact. Its Web site has an online carbon emissions calculator designed especially for young consumers.

## Web Sites

Due to the changing nature of Internet links, Rosen Publishing has developed an online list of Web sites related to the subject of this book. This site is updated regularly. Please use this link to access the list:

http://www.rosenlinks.com/ycf/sssg

# For Further Reading

Callard, Sarah, and Diane Millis. *Green Living: A Practical Guide to Eating, Gardening, Energy Saving and Housekeeping for a Healthy Planet*. London, England: Carlton Books Ltd., 2001.

David, Laurie. *Stop Global Warming: The Solution Is You!* Golden, CO: Fulcrum Publishing, 2006.

E Magazine. *Green Living: The E Magazine Handbook for Living Lightly on the Earth*. New York, NY: Plume (Penguin Group), 2005.

Hailes, Julia. *The New Green Consumer Guide*. New York, NY: Simon & Schuster, Ltd., 2007.

Lockwood, Georgene, and Carol Abel. *Complete Idiot's Guide to Simple Living*. Indianapolis, IN: Alpha Books, 2000.

Smith, Alicia Marie. *50 Plus One Tips for Going Green*. Chicago, IL: Encouragement Press, 2008.

Trask, Crissy. *It's Easy Being Green: A Handbook for Earth-Friendly Living*. Layton, UT: Gibbs Smith, 2006.

# Bibliography

Clean Air–Cool Planet. "A Consumer's Guide to Retail Carbon Offset Providers." December 2006. Retrieved December 2007 (http://www. cleanair-coolplanet.org/ConsumersGuidetoCarbonOffsets.pdf).

eHow Culture and Society editor. "How to Organize a Boycott." Retrieved January 2008 (http://www.ehow.com/how_135682_ organize-boycott.html).

England, Lizabeth. "Socially Responsible Business: Doing the Right Thing." U.S. Department of State, Bureau of Educational and Cultural Affairs, Business Ethics. Retrieved December 2007 (http://exchanges.state.gov/FORUM/JOURNAL/bus5background. htm#socially).

Go Petition Pty, Ltd. "How to Start a Petition." Retrieved January 2008 (http://www.gopetition.com/create.php).

Government Purchasing Project. "Don't Be Fooled: The Limits of Eco-Labels." Center for Study of Responsive Law. January 1996. Retrieved December 2007 (http://www.gpp.org/energy_ideas/ EI.0196/EI.0196.09.html).

Green Guide. "Bathroom Surface Cleaners." *National Geographic*. Retrieved January 2008 (http://www.thegreenguide.com/products/ Housekeeping/Bathroom_Surface_Cleaners).

Kalmanovitch, Michael. "Celebrating 16 Years of Community." Earth's General Store. Retrieved December 2007 (http://www.egs.ca).

Mello, Felicia. "Labels Help Consumers Decide if Carbon Footprint Fits." *Chicago Tribune*, September 23, 2007, p. 3A.

Nijhuis, Michelle. "Give It Away, Give It Away, Give It Away Now." Grist. May 17, 2004. Retrieved December 2007 (http://www.grist.org/news/maindish/2004/05/17/nijhuis-freecycle).

Smith, Lyrysa. "Let the Buyer Be Aware." *Times Union* (Albany, NY), May 31, 2004, p. C1.

Szewczyk, Matt. "How Can We Help Stop Global Warming Article: Using Recycled Paper Instead of Virgin Paper." Retrieved January 2008 (http://www.acoolerclimate.com/Articles/PreventGlobalWarmingPaperRecyclingFacts.html).

Terrapass. "How Carbon Offsets Work." Retrieved December 2007 (http://www.terrapass.com/about/how-carbon-offsets-work.html).

# Index

## A

Adopt-a-Supermarket, 36

## B

bags
    paper vs. plastic, 23
    reusable cloth, 23
boycott, organizing a, 37–38
bulk, buying items in, 29

## C

cacao farming in the Amazon, 19
carbon footprint
    explained, 5
    of goods/services, 9–11, 16, 20
carbon labels on products, 11
carbon offsets
    buying, 12–14
    explained, 12
Carbon Trust, 9
carpooling, 29
Certified Organic labels, 18, 19
chemical-free goods, 18–21
Clean Air–Cool Planet, 12
cleaning products, natural and organic,
    19, 33
Climate Trust, 14
clothing, and chemicals, 19–20
conspicuous consumption
    explained, 25
    tips for avoiding, 26
Co-op America, 36

cooperative living, 27–29
cooperative markets, 17

## D

decomposing items, and greenhouse gas
    emissions, 10, 21, 31
"disposable society," U.S. as a, 21
do-it-yourself (DIY) approach, 31–32
dry cleaning, chemicals used in, 19–20

## E

eco-responsible products, consumer
    demand for, 14–15, 38
electronics, upgrading, 32–33

## F

farmers' markets, 17
fertilizers/pesticides, use of, 19
freecycling, 29–31

## G

global warming, explained, 4–5
green consumer advocate, becoming a,
    34–38
greenhouse effect, explained, 4
greenhouse gases, 4, 7, 11, 18, 19, 21,
    23, 38

## I

impulse purchases, resisting, 26
"inconspicuous consumer," becoming a,
    25–33

## About the Author

Jeanne Nagle is a writer and editor living in upstate New York. She has a longstanding interest in environmental issues and is a member of Care of God's Creation, a grassroots environmental group in her area. Among the many titles she's written for Rosen Publishing are *Reducing Your Carbon Footprint at School* and the forthcoming *In the News: Living Green.*

## Photo Credits

Cover (top) Photo Alto/James Hardy/Getty Images; cover (middle) Mario Tama/Getty Images; cover (bottom) Monika Graff/Getty Images; p. 5 Justin Sullivan/Getty Images; pp. 7, 10 Scott J. Ferrell/Congressional Quarterly/Getty Images; p. 8 Peter Cade/The Image Bank/Getty Images; pp. 13, 16, 18, 35 © AP Images; p. 20 David McNew/Getty Images; p. 22 Mario Ruiz/Time & Life Pictures/Getty Images; p. 24 © Jame Pickerell/The Image Works; pp. 25, 28 Robert Nickelsberg/Getty Images; p. 27 Tim Boyle/Getty Images; p. 32 © Jeff Greenberg/The Image Works; pp. 34, 37 © www.istockphoto.com/Sean Locke.

Designer: Les Kanturek; Editor: Peter Herman
Photo Researcher: Cindy Reiman